LAND MARKS

LAND MARKS

poems

SHARON TRACEY

SHANTI ARTS PUBLISHING
BRUNSWICK, MAINE

LAND MARKS

Published by Shanti Arts Publishing
Designed by Shanti Arts Designs

Cover image by Sharon Tracey and used with her permission.

Shanti Arts LLC
193 Hillside Road
Brunswick, Maine 04011
shantiarts.com

Printed in the United States of America

ISBN: 978-1-956056-62-4 (softcover)

Library of Congress Control Number: 2022947816

for John

The land gets inside us;
and we must decide one way or another
what this means, what we will do about it.

—Barry Lopez

Contents

I

I Have Eaten Geographies

Hard bits and soft pieces,
bitter, sour, and sweet
places that have talked back,
made me who I am,
made me ache from too much—
whittled me.

What we love, we love.

I have sipped from a cenote,
bitten a spur, savored fine strata
near the mouth of a river.
Swallowed decades of dust,
mere motes
in the soul of an eon.

I have settled in a valley
between green hills. Given birth
to a daughter in a world of a billion
daughters. Given birth to two sons
in a world of a billion sons.
I have sun-dried my hands.

Rumi said there are a thousand ways
to kneel
and kiss the ground.

I have lost count. I am counting.

Prairie Dropseed and Me

As for man, his days are as grass
—Psalm 103:15 (ASV)

I have fallen for the ones
spilling forth in fountains

of flowered panicles, June's green
now autumn's copper

and I'm lying here with them
at eye-level—looking through

bronze to sky blue—
and close-up,

one way to see everything
quiver and fall

as the chickadees in black caps come
to snack and keep good company.

And though I want to believe in
beginnings and endings

I can never accept November
as the last ones

are eaten or buried
and the world keeps recycling

cruelty and beauty in equal measure,
and we keep hoping

for more of the latter, even
the smallest seed.

An Early Hour Is a Good Hour

In the cold dawn, the cottontails have emptied themselves
from the dense thicket of Russian olives
lining the driveway.

They race into the headlights
then freeze
like dewdrops on grass tips,
chopping the quiet up.

I pause so they can finish
what they've started.

An early hour is a good hour
to talk to cottontails
and ask why god has made
some perfect.

I study their grey rabbit faces,
the eyes sent to the sides
of their heads,
their coats and soft napes,
their lack of pretense.

I consider the habits we each have formed
for early morning, overlapping
in our orbits,
repetition a key
that opens a door.

Derek Drove the John Deere Tractor

Derek drove the John Deere tractor
to the house this morning
to mow the small field in the side yard,

and in doing so, freed
the trunk of the old red maple
from ferns, brambles, and goldenrod.

It now rises unencumbered

limbs sheathed in greater lengths of lichen,
a second skin, more minted. I bend
to pick up the broken ones,

carry the thick ribs
bleached by sun to the edge
and return to hug Old Red.

Under the living branches it smells like old man.

Some things are not fully describable.
But we can stand with an old tree and weep,
breathe in the sour air.

First Anniversary

Not the usual Tax Day, not the usual
middle spring, the surfeit of daffodils,
but something new. We stand inside
the month, a middle room, the days
too blurred to count, no door
with knob to turn. But stars still
wake me in the middle of the night,
the mourning doves in fog-grey
coats still warn. *In a pandemic,* my love
says, *try to hold only one day at a time.*
So today, on the first anniversary
of the Notre Dame inferno,
we watch on video as a man climbs
the south tower of the cathedral
to toll the ancient bell, Emmanuel
(God is with us). Jump-starts the heart
for the medics, the dead, and the sick.
Its toll reminds me of the people I forgot
to kiss, the arguments I once thought mattered.
Years ago, we stood there, not knowing
it had survived the Plague. The mourning
doves circling the spire no longer there.

Reasons to Praise the Ladybird Beetle

Because multitudes congregate in sunlit
corners, red elytra bright as embers.

Because they hide beauty in transparent wings
then unfold them like origami.

Because arrival seems so uncertain.
Because the field and garden grow tired of waiting.

Because there is no patron saint of insects.

Because who would not wish for blessings for the little ones,
seven spots for seven joys and seven sorrows.

Because it is the Virgin Mary's beetle.

Because when swarms of aphids devoured the crops
in the Middle Ages, she sent them.

November Aubade

The field not mowed and I am not unmoved
as autumn leaf-clouds waft
and I hear the far-off call
of a great-horned owl.
It's barely light,
the field not ours to own.

What passes at this hour,
what graces to behold—

I take my coffee black
and sit within
the doorway
and watch violet whales
drift overhead

not indifferent
to the letting go—

Are we not animals,
impermanent
as clouds?

The Field behind the House

If you find yourself
falling in love
with a particular one—
its furrowed brow
and branching logic,
its gold-stemmed grasses
and earth the hue
of prunes,
its sprigs of redbuds
stiffer than brooms,
and clumps of
blue wild iris,
maybe go with it.
The land hums
though we may not
know its hymns.
We can try to sing
them anyway.

Bittersweet

I follow the prickled path it wends round
trunk and limb, twining and climbing,
its yellow-capsuled red fruit a hard pill
to swallow. The afternoon is quiet and all
I see is aftermath—how it has made itself
with swarming, surviving with a bitter
warmth. The beauty marks track decline
in these grey woods. Today, I've come
with pruning shears to cut a crown and crop
twisted strands for wreath and winter bower.
What is lost? We sometimes come to save
what needs no saving. While the woods
accept the bittersweet.

The Work of Some Asemic Writers

Yesterday, stacking
a cord of hardwood
for next winter
I found reams of messages
scrimshawed
not on whalebone
but imprinted
on a dozen split logs,
hieroglyphic heavings
in sigils and scribbles,
the scrollwork
of bark beetles
so lovely
it's hard to believe
they are killing
the trees
as they drill through
the dark.
I set the inscribed
pieces aside,
spines facing out
as if I can read them,
think of the pyres
of books, the languages
never learned
before burning.

Walk in the Driving Rain

Mud is the medicine these days, it seems
the rain won't leave us well enough alone
and its sharp drops have now congealed to fill
an open tomb with lake. No measured dose,
it smells like death and so I grieve, pull on
my boots, and take the well-worn path I know,
across the tracks to reach beyond the curve,
and there it sits above the ooze, makeshift
bridge without a name, with footholds and a
wooden rail to grasp above the drowning
world. *Listen.* Can you hear the beavers splash—
slap as they work? Stripping bark for spare parts
to build a dome above their water door,
spackling to protect the womb, to warm.

The Dryer, the Birds, and the Plumber

The plumber cut a hole in the drywall
and yanked it from forty feet
of plastic tubing—a clutch
of feathers and remnants of nests
laced with clumps of dryer lint.

He names them by feather type: kestrel,
grackle, thrush, red-tailed hawk—
has a story for each,
is in no rush
to finish the work.

The laundry room smelled
like putrid eggs
so I purchased lavender
dryer sheets
to flower-scent the place
but he says,
Toss them, they're endocrine disruptors,
real killers, and who am I
to argue with a bird-loving plumber.

He asks me for baby powder
and then shakes it
into the tubing
and blasts the blow dryer,
infusing the room
with warmth until it smells
like a nursery, that sweet cradle-cap.

For his final act—
he ascends the ladder I left leaning against the house
and nails a mesh-metal screen
over the exhaust vent
to keep future fledglings out.
One small fix in a broken world,
but something.

One Hairy Woodpecker

In the morning
under the eaves
I find him
as if asleep.
Already, the ants
are busy at work.

I scan the yard
for a fitting burial site,
grab a shovel from the garage
and dig a small grave
in the garden,
somewhere between
deep and shallow.

He's handsome—
black and white
with a crimson splash
on his head
and a chisel-like bill,
which helps identify him.
He's considered
a species of "least concern."

I lay him to rest
with a handful of summer
buttercups.
Scan a few dead trees for kin
who might sing for him.

The River and the Oxbow

This is not the famous vista
of the Connecticut painted
by Thomas Cole, a bird's-eye
view of the oxbow
in all its convolution,
nor the story of its long journey
south through four New England states
as it carves its course,
hundreds of tributaries joining
along the way to form
a country called watershed.

This is just a quarter-mile-slate-blue
swath of river at the end of a small road
containing just enough of itself
that I think I can come to know it.
From this vantage point
there's no way to see the oxbow
meandering a few miles south of here,
even though I know it keeps growing,
have felt the power
of land, have heard it say,
Settle down. Stay.

After Hopkins

Late afternoon on Route 9, I'm giving thanks
for dappled light on the stream of cars
stopping for gas at Cumberland Farms,

for the Liberty Tax man dancing curbside
in his mint green costume with a free class sign.
I wave and wait for green at that dumb light

near Spirithaus, where men load silver kegs
into minivans, and the windows of Florence Bank
gleam like diamond panes. I'm giving thanks

for glitter on newborn trees at the local nursery
and puddles in the used-car parking lot
reflecting the glow of a red pickup truck

and the yellow school bus heading west
with its flashing lights and windshield glare
as Hopkins's "fresh-firecoal" words rise up:

all things counter, original, spare, strange

Roadside Haiku I

clouds scurry and part
kestrel perched on the roof ridge
roots hold a rainstorm

II

In the Country of the Pointed Firs

*There is a place remote and islanded, and given
to endless regret or secret happiness.*
—Sarah Orne Jewett

We hiked the island, shaped like a maple
seed and brushed with wild blueberries,

crunched stones along the carriage paths
then climbed the crest of Cadillac Mountain.

A raft of clouds sailed by. A crew of hawks.
Blue pierced the day with its harpoon—I swear

I saw a breaching whale. I could see the land
bridge far below, the narrows sharp and cold,

and everywhere we turned, the pointed firs.
No tree is a country. No woman an island.

We drive off, and yet, things follow.
The world turns darker blue.

Geography of H

H is for horizons and hoodoos,
for hills, hooks, and hollows.
For hogback and horseback,
for hot springs and hardpan.
H is for history and hemispheres,
for hearth and for heaven,
for haves and have-nots, for
hardwoods and howlers.
H is for heartlands, highlands,
and hinterlands. For headwalls,
hamlets, and hanging valleys.
H is for hummocks, hammocks,
and hedgerows. For habits and
habitats, for haystacks and hassocks.
H is for headlands and harbors,
for houses and hours. For hell
and horn, for hate and hunger.
H is for hailstorms, and always,
that thing with feathers.

After Hopper

There was something
I could never name—a gauze,

a permeated pause
caught between comfort and alert.

A wave curled between beach grass
and the empty porch.

Afternoon amber, Cape reflection.
A trace of gold threaded the windows.

A white house with two chimneys,
a grand dame on her own glassy hill.

She shivered in a skirt of curtains,
accepted the cold kiss of the sun.

What is out of reach?

A cloud passed.
I stood alone and felt the ocean.

The Outermost House

Here is the house
that Henry Beston built in '25
and came to
in solitude
a humble house with windows
on all sides
to be with the birds,
the fish, the pinpoint stars.

Set in the dunes
and later left
to fight the wind
and encroaching sands.

A lonely-looking humble house.

In '76, we visit in daylight
then wait for night, a chance
to drag our sleeping bags
between two crests of dune
nestled near the house.

Crawl in, the light a crescent moon.

Listen as the waves swash
a messy line
between two worlds.

Who knew the blizzard of '78
would come
in two short years
to take the humble house away
for good
like anyone or any house

what is lived will wash away—

Passing through on the New Jersey Turnpike

Without the stream of cars at this early hour, past
the oil tank farms, the factories, the overhead cranes,
the American Dream Ferris Wheel, and the Fastlane,
the Meadowlands seem eerily peaceful, the earth

barely stirred, gilded in reed and cordgrass, river dredge
and landfill. Smokestacks emit cream-colored steam
that slowly curdles as we near the exit of my youth.

At this early hour, the New York City skyline casts
an opal glow on cargo containers stacked to the brow
of a cloud. There's a verdigris sheen on the bay,
a flash of jersey red tomato on a passing van.

The Atlantic white cedars are long gone. I once lived here
I tell my heart as we pass near the place of my birth
and not far from where my parents grew up.

There are many houses and sisters, a brother.
Childhood linked along a daisy chain of avenues
and towns, the Erie-Lackawanna train the background
rumble. We live together and apart, walk through

divorce into different griefs, follow different paths,
arrival a continuous state of reach. I think how
mercy tastes like nothing if not the driest leaves.

Houses rise and fall and are extended. They nest
inside us like Russian dolls, each in a particular
place. We dream. We build and destroy, work to
restore. To the east, giant pylons bask in sunlight,

the latticed steel etched to sky, the power lines
strung between them like silver chains as we drive
by, vow to make amends next time, to forgive

and to love. I think of taking the long route
home to make time for a visit, but the sun is rising,
the traffic growing, and I want to believe we
all have miles and miles to go before we sleep.

On Nauset Beach

The birds have come and gone
and here in the sand
lie their arrows
telling time without a face,
soft signatures
the tide will soon erase
and maybe for this
I love them even more.

The morning sky is scratched
with seagulls, and seven seals
poke glossy heads above
the swells,
and I have walked far
through fulvous beachgrass
to reach this shore,
cold grains of sand
pressed firm against my heel.

This earth we claim as ours.
From here, walk east
and drown,
or aim your arrows elsewhere
and perhaps you too
will find a place
you forgot you loved.

Before Autopsy at the Smithsonian Museum of Natural History

—in memory of a North Atlantic Right Whale

You died and all the parts my heart had seen, you touched.
I think of that time now. Virginia on a late November
afternoon. I did not see you come. I don't remember
how we lifted you, all fifty tons onto the flatbed truck.
Heaved your blackened back, some rope. I was young,
riding shotgun back to Washington DC, past Jefferson
and Lincoln, the frosted gingered grass along the Mall.
At a traffic light on Constitution Ave, we stopped.
The people in the crosswalk paused and turned to stare.
The light changed. We drove on and reached the loading dock
and entered there, below the floors with pearly rows
of skeletons and specimens stretched high and low,
collecting yellow dust, a silent must. Why do you strand?
Of understanding no one spoke. The cetologists brought
out the knives. And all the while your secret smell I stood
and took, in my black boots and winter coat.

The Cherry Blossoms

The National Cherry Blossom Festival was canceled
but nobody told the Yoshino cherry trees.

The Potomac Tidal Basin quieter
than usual,

a silver bowl of rising waters
inside a ring of pink trees.

The world an open catacomb—

satellite images revealing new contours
of the earth, cleared for a moment of exhaust   paused

while black from the dampness
they who have reached peak bloom

on the twentieth day of the third month,
cold frames of cherry wood, fragrant

spreading crowns—

how they dust themselves.

Prophetic clocks, they will not stop
for pandemic or church bell.

A lone woman plays the violin,
a man kneels near a trio of trees

the reflections echo—

Changing Times

A traveler's road
solitude within a crowd
you could see through
no one could find you
a bus spanned the distance
the land seemed wider
the hours longer
no one asked
was it simpler
was it harder
did you read maps
were you lonely
afraid of strangers
the fact is
we are older
every moment
were the days longer
or do these days
seem shorter
what is it
that we keep
the rain thrashing stronger
the storms longer
the warm warmer

Crossing State Lines

vacuoles of fog
filling in
casting off
liminal shine
tissue of sky
dissolving
lane shifts
road marks
yellow white
condensing
molecules
peering out
discerning
a fragile vagility
out of shadows
almost missing
crossing over
invisible border
highway sign
Welcome

The Bluefish, the Birds, and the Fisherman

—Cape Hatteras National Seashore

The fisherman held a handful of bluefish
like a bouquet
of upside-down flowers.
He offered us one. It was early March,
the human offseason.

We built a fire in the cool sand
and cooked the fish,
ate as we watched
the fisherman recast his line
into the surf.

We had peddled south that day
camping gear packed in panniers,
stopping now and then
to watch the birds arriving
in the flush of their busiest season—

Black Skimmers, Stilts, and the Avocets
with milk-blue legs.

As darkness fell, the fisherman packed up his gear
and nodded in our direction. We bowed
to the bluefish and the birds,
breathed in what was tossed up
by the old ocean.

Vaccine Research at the St. Charles Laboratory

Blue blood drips into clear glass bottles
as the horseshoe crabs are bled—
picture cerulean
or the wing of a chalkhill blue—
and still the photo startles the way
I once jumped up after sitting on a cactus,
needles penetrating deep beyond
seven layers of skin—
and though I've heard of the practice,
it did not *register*, I mean
I didn't understand
what it meant to be inside—
hundreds of them,
tipped like army helmets in long single files
in perfect formation, immobile
in their sacrifice
as the blue blood is drawn,
or shall we say *withdrawn*
not like the pretty vial of ruby
I gave this week
to have my counts worked up,
self-satisfied and a little bit sick.
No, this is serious business
and too late to look away
to say, *I had no idea*
as they extract the precious blue blood
from a vein near the heart,
and after a few days, throw them
back into the ocean saying, *they'll be fine.*

The Glassblower

She spins a sky-blue globe
with a blowpipe,
silica, soda ash, limestone
and extreme heat.

From the first furnace, pulls
a crucible of molten glass, then
into the second, keeps turning it
so the glass stays soft
as the marver shapes it.

The process requires her breath.
Staccato shards crackle
beneath her boots as she steps.

With calipers, she carries the fragile vessel
to the annealing oven.

While we wait for the cooling,
the champagne cowboys are racing
to the edge of space,
red rockets burning gold above
billions on earth.

This old brick building was once a church.
I gaze out the high arched window,
hear the faint song of falling birds.

Open Road

Above us, close-knit families in sky-swarms,
others in delicate V's, and a few waifs

and strays scatter along the edge of flyway
as we drive below in two-lane formation,

leading lines in parallel of earth and air.
Above the engine whirs, honks of snow geese

and impatient drivers merge. Margin
of horizon stirs as green highway signs

in Helvetica fast approach and disappear.
The road splits the land in two, a backbone

through a middle earth as we speed on,
suspended between here and there

as the snows swerve south without
a crossroads, the world blurring in cloud.

Roadside Haiku 2

parsley-green glass bits
reflect the edges of dusk
crushed by a Jeep wheel

III

There Was Nothing but Land, Not a Country at All

There was nothing but land, not a country at all,
but the material out of which countries are made.
—Willa Cather

Where no one thing or person
blocks the view—
where you can almost fold
the sky and land in two

the grasslands a sea—
the sky-wind blowing through—
Prairie is her name or call her
Plains if you prefer.

She goes about her modest business.
Needs no preacher man to wash her
sins away.

When I stepped off the bus
in Western Nebraska
I tried to take everything in.
The scope and prospect. The solace.

But nothing is simple.
Some things are too vast—
I stood there with Prairie.
Closed my eyes and listened.

Midpoint

—Lebanon, Kansas

Between two, always another.
Tunneling in, magnifying.
As we move closer, we move farther.

In. Out. In.

The car thumps, a heartbeat on concrete.
The head holds the invisible map.
Hands steer the heart.

About two miles northwest of town
You can find the historical marker,
The geographical center of a contiguous country.

You can sign the guest register and leave a note
There's even a tiny white chapel,
A place to contemplate the center of things.

The way forward is inside.
Or maybe it's outside on the road.
Leaving town I couldn't help but look back—

Anchored to a mirage of terra firma,
Atoms of field-lake-cloud in different phases.
All of us matter, all of us burning stars.

Day of Repose

It was a Sunday. Robin egg blue, cool.
The sward was green. The hayfield windrowed.
It was late summer. Mammals were being mammals.
Trees were being trees. Breathing and leaning.
There was a soccer field behind a school.
A Main Street with a hardware store.
A white church with a slate steeple.
It was quiet. There were few early risers.
There was a closed gas station. A café was open.
There was a *Help Wanted* sign. I bought a coffee.
There was a great distance. A transmission of light.
There was a beech, a blanket, and a book.
We stayed all day. It was no time at all.

Geography of F

F is for flatirons, folds, faults,
and fractures. For false passes,
feldspar, and fossil beds.
F is for fissures and fumaroles,
for free fall, fervor, and flame.
F is for field, fen, and forest,
for finger drifts of snow, frozen
candles, and frost hollows.
F is for flint, flux, and fork,
for flutes, freshets, and fjords.
For fogbanks and flotsam, for
flashpoints, floes, and foment.
F is for flatwoods and floodplains,
for foothills, fertility, and futility.
F is for the faithful and faithless,
for all feathered things.

Pipeline

pipe sections
laid out
pan pipes
pretty aqua-blue
on old snow
the mule deer
frozen
stare at us
something about
lengthy
preparations
partners
in prosperity
tar sands
and crude
something about
whooping
cranes and wolves
snow a stiff sea
the mule deer
motionless
gelid eyes
mule-sized ears
hear more
than we know

Dear Rachel Carson,

The snow geese keep coming
I am sorry to report, from the north
heading south, white as refined sugar
with their soft black wingtips

flying through clouds near Butte,
over frozen fields of razed corn
near the old Anaconda Copper Mine,
flocks thick as snowflakes, thousands

of partners for life, touching down
on pools of jade.

There is a dark dream I'm driving
on an empty highway, searching
for signs of the Superfund site
so I can warn them, but

I always wake too soon.

In Arches National Park

In the table of hardness
  known as the Mohs scale
    talc is scratched by fingernail,
      feldspar will scratch gypsum
        but not quartz, which will in turn
          scratch apatite but not corundum.
        None will touch diamond.
        A hierarchy for everything.
          For beauty, I'll take the ones low
          on the scale, the sedimentary
            grains of sand, silt, and clay
              held together more loosely,
                that begin their journey as
                  sediments carried in rivers
                  and come to rest in the beds
              of lakes and oceans, layer
            upon layer of striated strata
          hued in sunrise tones
        of lavender and violet-grey,
      of reddish clay and sage,
      and maybe I'm sentimental
    but their transitory nature
    more quickly worn and hewn
  seems otherworldly as they
  succumb to the godly winds
in the daily work of weathering—
whittling hoodoos, pinnacles, and
windows in the souls of rocks—
spanning and opening

One Afternoon in Los Alamos

After visiting the pueblo dwellings
carved into tuff rock at Bandolier,
and having walked far under
a cloudless sky in August,
our family found a Baskin-Robbins
on Trinity Drive
and stepped into darkness.
No electricity. Can't save them, the boy
behind the counter said,
meaning the ice cream cakes
in pastel pinks, garish mint,
and bubblegum blue, beading
as they glistened, the ten-gallon tubs
slowly melting in pools.
You may ask why is this a poem.
Take whatever you want
is what the boy said, and so
we chose triple cones
and ice cream cakes
and found a shaded place,
the ice cream melting faster
than we could slurp and savor.
Only in the aftermath did it occur
to me that we were mere miles
from where they built the atomic bomb
and where Oppenheimer chose
the codename *Trinity* for the test site,
inspired by Donne's holy sonnet,
Batter my heart, three-person'd God.
What burning star will take us?

In Abiquiú

God told me if I painted it enough, I could have it.
—Georgia O'Keeffe

She's talking about the mountain, the one
she could see from her studio at Ghost Ranch,
the one who accepted her ashes
after her death.

Mountain ground—
where she could settle down
with the skulls and bones
of horses, cows, and calico roses.

The days pass. A stockpile
of stones and red rocks, cottonwoods
cut here and there by dry canyon.
The road dusted.

A wild chokecherry place.
A cooler filled with drinks wedged
between the kids
in the back seat of a Jeep.

Sometimes you just need to stop
and step out,
tell yourself: *look*
Look deeper.

Sunrise Run in Zion

she's dinging the clouds   she's dabbing at switchbacks
banging on boulders   the doors of rock squirrels

she carries a slingshot   a bag full of pebbles
she's making them tremble   she loves to make trouble

another ricochet—

she's pacing herself   she's splicing pink ribbons
on cliffs of carnelian   she's burnishing sandstone

the scruff of the sagebrush   the muzzles of mule deer
she's rising then spilling   down into the canyon

she's boring a hole with her light   trying to reach
where the rattlesnakes sleep   she can sense them

you can't stop her—

she climbs faster than you   can run up the trail
spreads out on a limb   she takes her sweet time—

It's summer in Springdale   it's barely called morning
the children are sleeping   a curtain is glowing

the bloom is the hour   two mothers are running—

Behind the Desert Pearl Inn

—Springdale, Utah

On the banks of the Virgin River
amid fluttering cottonwoods

and the white heat of a summer
afternoon, violet waters streaming

a steady beat of background music,
my daughter kneels and scoops

handfuls of red clay from riverbank
to build a small adobe house

where scarab, blister, and darkling
beetles might come and play. I watch

as she polishes the floor with slick mud
and casts the courtyard with a private sun.

I didn't realize until later when I found
the photo I thought I had lost, that this

was the cusp at the end of a childhood.
Stay here with us for a while as the tiny

house dries and she adorns the door
with the yellow rays of brittlebush.

Easter Weekend in Sedona

I woke green as a praise song—
was risen in that box canyon,
bands of old ocean marking the way

in millions, the Colorado Plateau
uplifted, the sandstone pinnacled
above the trail as we entered

the open-air cathedral. A raptor's caw
cut the quiet inside the red-rock walls.
A trinity of dove-white clouds unfurled

across the blue. Then the rush of liquid
air, lifted high the leaves of manzanita,
exposing hard limbs, chestnut-hued.

I thought of all the arms. Of nail
and wood, dead soldiers and civilians.
I tasted salt and dust on my skin.

The horror of another war lay hidden
in the canyon shadows. The god of rocks
was silent. This ministry was all wind.

What the Poverty Grass Said on Route 66

You can count on me
to keep growing   worn-out
in modest poverty

sprouting though exhausted
in no mixed company   with the rich
the ones   swallowing their loam

my spikelets & twisted awns
jutting out   into the sour sky
of lemon clouds

defying God to kill me
to call me by my Latin name—
          Danthonia spicata

to stamp me out.

Until then—

if you are homeless   come
if you have humble hands   come
if you have rambling hopes   come

pick *me* gather me up
make a mattress tick   to rest
your bones

lay down your burdens
in any state along
this Mother Road.

Notes after Meeting the Saguaros in the Sonoran Desert

That they reach for clouds.
That to some, they seem human.
That they might nick a thunderhead

and bring the rain. That they grow
mere inches in long years.
That a century is middle-aged.

That every trunk provides a home
for someone or something.
That they offer elf owls safe harbor.

That their ribs are made of wood.
That some never grow arms
and yet, still they hold things.

That they are a keystone species,
providing food and shelter.
That come spring, they wear crowns

of cloud-white flowers. That open
at night. That bloom for one day.
That wait for bat, bird, insect.

That they can never walk away.

Waiting in Line to Be Added
to the Endangered Species List

No cooler climes coming. Too many
standing in line. They have filed papers,

submitted facts and figures. Stamped
forms in anticipation of an opening.

Who knows how long the Joshua trees
will wait? Members of the Yucca tribe,

the old ones remember being born
on the high desert, on a cool morning

in spring after the rainstorm when poppies
bloom and spread their buttered faces.

The prophets raise their tired arms to pray.
The people sleep, the fires burn.

Fuel for the Fire

Eucalyptus scrolls of pink-green bark,
the crackle and pop of cottonwoods, pitch
pines, and pin oaks. Forests of falsehoods
and scattering flocks, herds of wild elk.
Sagebrush and cheatgrass, fences and
neighbors, barnyards and stables, anger
and arrogance tied up with twine and tossed
with the bales. Wildflowers and seeds
adrift in wind, hate with its small teeth,
crowds of believers in seasonal colors
and all creeds. Laundry forsaken on
a clothesline. Headwinds and tailwinds
and greed. Two-legged creatures who
like to kick horses. Rage that stampedes.

Roadside Haiku 3

scenic overlook
scorched skeletons on the slope
yellow danger sign

IV

After the Wildfire

Where are the dental records for the deer,
the mountain lion, the September cubs
born in the shade of the ceanothus
in the foothills north of Los Angeles?
Where are the records for the blue-eyed
bobcat, the gray fox? The California quail
with its sporty plume who would rather
run than fly, the underbrush its palace.
When the smoldering died down, we hiked
the hills and searched for signs of life
in the riparian rubble. Scoured a path
through scorched scrub oak. Heard no growl,
no whirring wing, no chatter. The stars
went out. The wind conspired with the fire.

Outside the Staples Center
in Downtown Los Angeles

Ravens fly over the new skyscrapers, cutting
the blue above S. Figueroa Street
and I want to know what they see
from that vantage point, what they eat,
what rodents are scurrying where the executive
helicopters land. I look around for green to touch
beneath the gleaming, beyond the people on the streets.
What reason for the inequality of days?
The ravens reel in loopy circles sixty stories
high. A monstrous crane slowly lowers
a row of men down the side of a skyscraper
to clean its eyes, the glass as bluish-green
as the sea, the air washed with the sound
of sirens a mile away, the homeless returning.

The Deployment of Bees

It used to be they could choose
their own hours   fields and flowers
but now many are forced
to commute
a beekeeper explained to me
over coffee
at a café near Fresno
how they travel on flatbed trucks
in winter

to almond orchards in the Central Valley
then south on I-5
to groves of avocado and fields
of broccoli
while some are sent
out-of-state to cherry trees
in Washington.

Since then, I can't stop thinking of them—
armies of hives on the interstate
stacked   row upon row
engines humming   thumping
wings

plucked from time and stuck   at rush hour.

Solo Hike on the Wilderness Coastal Trail

—Olympic National Park

I walk beside the slosh-talking
median strip of sea-beach—
listening to surf-speech
stepping over long bones

of driftwood, clumps of kelp
hanging their copper hair
on blue rocks. The birds
are black turnstones.

I cross wet headlands, slipping
on skins of banana slugs.
I've just washed my long hair
with a gallon of spring water,

eldest daughter who has read
both Bible and the tidal charts, who
thinks she saw the face of God
in the Pacific near Cape Alava.

I reach the petroglyphs at low tide—
whale and hunter-faces carved
long ago by the Makah tribe. With
a stone, bone, or wooden maul

it's hard to tell. This place is called
Wedding Rocks. Why I wonder—
so many seem to arrive alone.
My mother said: go, don't call me.

Driving up Haleakalā, House of the Sun

Cherry-colored trucks and pickups rust
as the sun torches a vacant
building, the field shorn of sugarcane,
a faded billboard so forlorn
it seems to say *I'm sorry*
before the car begins to climb
and we pass him—
a bronzed man carrying a six-foot white cross
on his right shoulder,
steadying it with Picasso-like hands
as he trudges uphill to the point
where earth, sea, and sky
form a perfect trinity.
Later, back home,
I won't mention him.
I'll talk about the humpbacks
breaching in Maalaea Bay,
my own pilgrimage
to the Merwin Palm Forest,
the hotshot surfers in Paia,
the silverswords on the summit
of the dormant volcano
where the air is thin. We breathe in
what we can breathe.
See what we choose to see.
I won't mention that clouds
conceal the pilgrim's road.

How Days Are Observed

God flew out of Logan to Copenhagen
on the same flight, sat in Economy
and neither of us had a window seat.
Boarded the same train into the heart
of the city. God said *walk with me*
into the square, under the plane trees,
each snug in a slow-release green
watering bag. And God threw words on
the cobblestones as the wheels of a thousand
bicycles passed, imprinting them like veins
on leaves. And the clouds slowly roused themselves,
throwing shadows as we traveled on to Bergen
where the seagulls screeched like Hitchcock's birds
and there was no way to stop them. Later, flying
home and given a window seat above the earth—
I could see nets strung like gossamer along the coast,
and only slowly realized they were holding pens
for farmed salmon. And the farmers were invisible
and the lives of the fish were invisible
and the sun lit the ripples of the North Sea
like lightning only there was no sound,
only the light on the surface separating us.

Godbird

Limosa limosa, you black-tailed
godwit, long-legged prober
migratory mud wader
you seem a god on speed
slurping up plump polychaetes
& mollusks to double your weight,
record holder for the longest flight
ever tracked by satellite—
New Zealand-China-Alaska

& back again—no changing planes
no baggage checked nor claimed
high-tailing it over the Mai Po Marsh
the Yellow River a squirt of murky mustard
glimpsed through smog as you soar
over soggy hills and bogs,
what full-steam-ahead stamina

no fear of flight like some of us
sitting in this chrome capsule
aloft on the other side of the world
cutting through cumulus & leaving contrails—
wondering how this makes any sense
gripping the armrest
& praying
keep us safe from ourselves

as the flight attendant
interrupts the beverage service
and calls us to attention—
please fasten your seatbelts
we are experiencing some turbulence

The Eallu

Time is not passing. Time is coming.
—Anders Oskal, secretary-general of the
Association of World Reindeer Herders

Oskal says, *we follow them,*
they don't follow us,
tundra or taiga,
the herders follow
the Eallu.
He reminds me that
light keeps coming
with the time
that is coming,
which I find reassuring
in a world of reindeer
being reindeer
and the herders following
as time keeps coming
to meet the reindeer.

Tonight, I'm giving up
the habit of always
looking back,
of adding up
the past.
I'm dreaming of reindeer
and counting.

Tonight, the winter sky
seems brighter.
Three sisters—
Alnitak, Alnilam, and Mintaka—
strung in a clique
of sparkling holes
in the belt of Orion
are sending their light
as time keeps coming
and the Eallu survive
on the lichens
as the permafrost thaws
and time keeps coming—

If I Knew His Name, I Would Write It Here

—after Sharon Olds, "A Song Near the End of the World"

Because I suddenly think of the elk—
doesn't mean the elk is near.
Time has passed since he has passed,
a half-ton giant in his copper coat. He who gave me
no heed as he lumbered by the wooded path
then held his ground as he held me
in equal gaze.
From fairest creatures we desire increase.
On his head he wore a crown—a rack
of many tines—covered in summer velvet.
He was like a god, hailing from the Genus
Cervus, a true star.
He harbored no gang or herd
and made his remarks directly on the hard earth.
I was no more than a shadow
on the far side of a screen door.
He was king and thus he held forth,
pausing now and then as he supped
on sweetgrass and forbs. Did I say
around his teeth he wore a wreath of sweet breath?
My fervent wish for him:
be fruitful and multiply, make safe passage to spring.
He bugled. I wished upon his star.

Autumnal Equinox, 2020

The sun slipped under houses,
one moment light,
then a finger's small poke
on the horizon
to start again the dark.

Animals understood except
for us who stayed inside,
somehow far less equipped.

We brace ourselves—
for days of shorter straws,
a maw that won't be sated
until the last drop is squeezed
and doled out.

Which should be no surprise
but we forget.
This is the world.

Gather up the children.
Be alert past twilight.
See that the deer have bedded down.
This is the world.
A half-cup of light, half-cup of dark.

Antarctica

I

Can we talk about the blue?
Clearest, truest, strongest,
pure glacier ice blue, the hue
that develops over time as newer ice
is worn away by wind and sublimation
and then, where light reaches in, penetrates more deeply.
The blue revealed—
compacted with few bubbles,
the air squeezed out by the sheer weight
of glacier, rock to vapor.
Altered in form but not essence,
an incarnation. A heavenly blue.

II

Two girls dive into the blue
frigid sea, and float there among
the brittle stars with long skinny arms,
floating as if in outer space,
then dive deeper still
but first, closer to the surface,
there's the rusted hull of a whaling ship
trapped in ice long ago that sunk
with harpooned whales on deck,
and I can see the girls
quiet and clear
above the whale fall, sad cathedral.
Any one of us might have been
someone else in a different life.

III

Twelve million penguins. There at the edge
at the end of the earth, maybe
with some god-given latitude
to be free. They with the afterfeathers.
What would you say is the afterlife?
Why assume heaven is above the sky?

To All the Starlings

To all the starlings making murmurations
above us, across sky-beams, yawning blue-shafts
exchanging air for feathers as if one organism,
to all the horses and other odd-toed ungulates
corralled or caught or pushed off stamps
of land, to all the cetaceans and crustaceans
traveling the oceans, beached, or taken to a lab,
to all the chickens, pigs, and other domestics,
the salmon and the sturgeon and other bony fish,
to all the wildcats in the world, to all the ants
of industry, to all egg-laying queens
washing themselves clean in moth light,
to the last red wolf and all the dogs—

If existence is the exchange is the music
is the water flowing down the light it catches
is the dripping of the sounds in evening gutters
if we are open and aware of all the others
if the exchange is the music is the stars
exploding—
            starlings starlings starlings
        starlings starlings starlings starlings starlings
    starlings starlings starlings starlings starlings starlings starlings
      starlings starlings starlings starlings starlings starlings
        starlings starlings starlings starlings starlings
          starlings starlings starlings starlings
            starlings starlings starlings
              starlings starlings
                starlings

The Palms in Haiku

I have never lived anywhere that was more true.
—W. S. Merwin

The way a place can be a poem,
another way to understand
the world as it comes tumbling out—
stars, seeds, a sea of shells
where the bodies have been lost.
One January, we flew to Maui
and journeyed to the town of Haiku,
where the poet had planted
thousands of palms—a forest
thick with fronds, bamboo, sour fruit,
and fermented seedpods. Tended them
for more than forty years. Heavy rains
had fallen but cleared that morning
as we walked among them
and came upon the nestled house,
close enough to spy a stack of books
perched on the porch railing
and marked with pink Post-it notes.
As if he will be back tomorrow.
Invisible birds are singing, leaflets
of palms sway in the trade winds.
The gardener has given each of us
a small handful of seeds.

In Leucadia

I

Some places proclaim themselves, speak the nature of things.
In Leucadia, *place of refuge,* there are streets named for Greek
gods—Hygeia, Hermes, and Hestia, Vulcan and Neptune.
Hodonyms I did not know. We had come for respite
and reunion and set down our hearth on Urania. There
are signs and crossings. The Pacific Surfliner streaking
up the Pacific Coast Highway with its organ-low whistle
while the slush of cars passes like waves. A traveler
might go anywhere. Here, the parking and beaches
are free. We stroll past public murals of lush flowers
and fish, watch streetscape construction that zings as
bulldozers carve trenches for new pipes and young trees.
Some things take years. Come evening, the moon tugged
the tides to the sandstone cliffs and no one cried.

II

If you came this way, cross-lit by sunset and lamplight,
bewitched or beset, the daze of summer's last days might
seep inside you too among the low-slung surf and taco shops,
the sea casting a numinous sheen on the surfers, seal-sleek
in their wetsuits, lolling on swells and poised for the next
set. Near dusk, a small crowd gathers on Neptune above
the sandstone cliffs to witness the marigold sun slowly
sink below the horizon, hoping to see the green flash.
An old man plucks the strings of his ukulele, playing
here comes the sun, even as it slips away, while behind us,
a cream moon rises imperfectly round. It's a five-minute
walk to Saint Archer's Brewery, where there's a weekly
bingo game to play. Alas, Apollo has no road here, no
place to set down his golden bow and silver arrows.

III

If you came this way, I could not name for you the divine.
I might only say that the marine layer of fog lifted its violet
self from the horizon before we arrived. That the days
of pandemic were so endless we lost ourselves inside it.
That the sky chipped itself, rinsed of color, of salt, of bird,
of rescue helicopter. That we long to return, to hold
each other again. One morning on Moonlight Beach
a child gathers giant kelp in a great pile, its curls
glinting like the hair of Venus, the strands washed by
saltwater and set to dry until the next high tide. One night
we witness spark lightning, then a mad rush of drops
that just as suddenly stops, too little to clear the hills
cloudy as cataracts. We lose sense of time. The distance
between hours, the treads between the living and the dying.

IV

If you came this way, you might see the yellow butterflies.
The old woman with flowing grey hair waxing her surfboard.
The middle-aged man opening the back door of his van
then pausing to wipe his feet on the Astroturf mat before
entering. Café workers scrubbing clean a dozen outdoor tables.
One morning, I met a Samoyed at the Nectarine Grove café,
far from his arctic homeland, attired in a fluffed double-coat
and ruff of fur, white as bleached coral. He stood there
like a god, commanding respect of the servers and those
being served. He was panting and only pretended
to smile. His black eyes held no disdain and held mine
for a spell. A young mother slowly approached with
a silver bowl of iced water and held it to his lips.
She refilled it. He drank for a very long time.

V

Some places proclaim themselves. Speak the nature of things.
One day, we climbed a slot canyon in the afternoon heat
and looked out over the Pacific, the land below us
draped in muslin, the I-5 humming like a fly.
I could see no master of the universe. It was too light
for stars. The days had slowly lost their numbers
but the air still held its cadence, its breath sweet
as sweat. There was no beginning or ending, no
need to carry report. The earth tracks its own time.
I looked out at the brown September hills, how
the grey-green pockets of sycamore, cypress,
and coastal oak bide their time. How they pin
themselves to a dryland and hope to survive.
To kneel was not nothing.

Notes

The epigraph comes from Barry Lopez's *Arctic Dreams*.

The famous view referred to in "The River and the Oxbow" is Thomas Cole's painting *View from Mount Holyoke, Northampton, Massachusetts, after a Thunderstorm – The Oxbow, 1836*. The Metropolitan Museum of Art, New York City.

"After Hopkins" includes a line from the Gerard Manley Hopkins poem "Pied Beauty."

The poems "Geography of H" and "Geography of F" were inspired by *Home Grown: Language for an American Landscape*, edited by Barry Lopez and Debra Gwartney. Also thanks to Emily Dickinson for "'Hope' is the thing with feathers."

T. S. Eliot's "East Coker" (*Four Quartets*) provided inspiration for "Passing through on the New Jersey Turnpike," and the last line of the poem echoes lines from Robert Frost's "Stopping by the Woods on a Snowy Evening."

"Before Autopsy at the Smithsonian Museum of Natural History" was inspired by a stranding and autopsy I once witnessed. The population of Northern Atlantic right whales (*Eubalaena glacialis*) is estimated to be fewer than 350 at the time of this writing (source: NOAA Fisheries website).

The poem title and epigraph, "There was nothing but land, not a country at all" comes from Willa Cather's novel *My Antonia*.

The open pit copper mines in Butte, Montana, are part of one of the largest Federal Superfund sites in the United States, designated in 1983. Remediation and cleanup are ongoing.

Abiquiú ("In Abiquiú") reflects the town's Tewa roots and is the Spanish translation of the Tewa word meaning "wild chokecherry place."

The poem "Outside the Staples Center in Downtown Los Angeles" was written before the Staples Center's name was officially changed on Christmas Day 2021 to Crypto.com Arena. The poem is sticking with the Staples Center name.

I have used a few phrases from Pliny the Elder's *Natural History Books 1-2* (translated by H. Rackham, revised and reprinted, 1949), including the reason for inequality of days (in "Outside the Staples Center in Downtown Los Angeles") and how days are observed (my poem of the same title).

The poem title "If I Knew His Name I Would Write It Here" is borrowed from a line in "North of Putney" by Libby Maxey. The italicized line is from Shakespeare's "Sonnet 1."

"The Eallu" was inspired by the article "In the Arctic, Reindeer Are Sustenance and a Sacred Presence" by Ligaya Mishan *(New York Times Magazine*, November 9, 2020).

"The Palms in Haiku" was inspired by a visit to W. S. Merwin's palm garden in Haiku, Maui. The epigraph is from the Merwin Conservancy website.

"In Leucadia" was inspired not only by the place, but by T. S. Eliot's "Little Gidding" *(Four Quartets).*

Acknowledgments

Many thanks to the editors of the following publications in which these poems first appeared, sometimes in slightly different forms.

Aji: "The Eallu," "Midpoint: Lebanon, Kansas," "There Was Nothing but Land, Not a Country at All"

Calliope Poetry and Bass River Press: A Farther Shore: Cape Cod Anthology: "The Outermost House"

Canary: "The Equinox, 2020," "Prairie Dropseed and Me," "Waiting in Line to Be Added to the Endangered Species List"

Lily Poetry Review: "Driving Up Haleakalā, House of the Sun"

Mom Egg Review: "Solo Hike on the Wilderness Coastal Trail"

Pirene's Fountain: "After the Wildfire," "Derek Drove the John Deere Tractor"

Radar Poetry: "Vaccine Research at the St. Charles Laboratory"

Silkworm: "The Deployment of Bees," "Fuel for the Fire," "What the Poverty Grass Said along the Edges of Route 66"

SWWIM Every Day: "I Have Eaten Geographies," "In the Country of the Pointed Firs"

Straw Dog Writers Guild Pandemic Poetry: "First Anniversary"

Terrain.org: "An Early Hour Is a Good Hour," "Outside the Staples Center in Downtown Los Angeles," "To All the Starlings"

The Banyan Review: "After Hopper," "Walk in the Driving Rain"

The Orchards Poetry Journal: "How Days Are Observed"

The Worcester Review: "Sunrise Run in Zion"

Tule Review: "Godbird"

I am grateful to be part of a vibrant writing community here in western Massachusetts. Special thanks to Jean Blakeman, Libby Maxey, Rebecca Hart Olander, and Adin Thayer for being my first readers and for Wednesday evenings filled with poetry, craft discussions, good food, and cake. Also deep thanks to Jane Andresen, Liesel de Boor, Beth Filson, Melenie Flynn, Kathy Ford, Mark Hart, and Paul Ita for writing group critiques and camaraderie.

We rarely journey alone—I am grateful to family and friends who have walked with me at some point along the way or provided inspiration. Also to Christine Cote for shepherding the book from design to publication. And my deepest thanks always to John, Kelly, William, and Samuel, for love and everything else.

SHANTI ARTS

NATURE · ART · SPIRIT

Please visit us online
to browse our entire book catalog,
including poetry collections and fiction,
books on travel, nature, healing, art,
photography, and more.

Also take a look at our highly regarded art
and literary journal, *Still Point Arts Quarterly*,
which may be downloaded for free.

www.shantiarts.com

www.ingramcontent.com/pod-product-compliance
Lightning Source LLC
Chambersburg PA
CBHW022036090426
42741CB00007B/1083